How to be Irish... Sure tis great craic!

By S. Daly

For questions and comments about this book,
please contact the author at
author.daly@mail.com

Hello there, how are ye? If you are one of them poor misfortunate creatures born outside the island of Ireland, then fear not, there are still a few things ye can do to be Irish. Follow the steps in this simple book and you'll be able to pass for a native in no time. So find a comfy spot, grab a pint of Guinness and soon (through a process known as osmosis) you'll be pissed and *havin the craic...*

For all my fellow Irishmen and women,
Sure aren't we gas out!

Table of Contents

Common Myths

So you want to be Irish eh? Well, who could blame you, sure aren't we only something else, to be fair to us. Anyway enough about us, how about you? Why do you want to be Irish? Are you visiting? Or perhaps you've won the genetic lottery and have some Irish blood in you. Either way, this is the book you need to read if you want to improve your understanding of all things Irish or if you want to avoid standing out like a pure edjet on your upcoming visit. So fear not, by the time you finish this book you'll be as Irish as meself, well almost.

Now the first thing to get out of the way is all them silly myths about Ireland and its people. Myths, fibs or old wives' tales (don't even ask) as they are called in Ireland refer to misconstrued global myths relating to the country.

So here I am going to list the most common ones so that you don't stand out like a sore thumb on your trip.

- ***Everyone says "Top of the morning to ya!"*** No! That is just wrong on so many levels.
- ***We eat lucky charms for breakfast.*** Nope, I'm pretty sure you can't even buy them here.
- ***All Irish women wear Claddagh rings.*** No Irish woman past the age of twelve would be caught dead wearing a Claddagh ring
- ***We all have red hair*** False, in fact just 10% of the population has red, auburn or strawberry blond hair. Redheads are

also affectionately referred to as gingers, carrot toppers or my personal favourite, ginger nuts, charming eh!

- ***Everyone here speaks Irish!*** Sure, you'll find the odd weirdo hidden in a ditch alongside the western shoreline who is a fluent Gaeilgeoir (Irish speaker) but the vast majority of us are unable or unwilling to string a sentence together.
- ***Irish dancing is the done thing on a night out.*** We don't be Irish dancing in the nightclub on a Saturday night unless you're in Leitrim.
- ***Leprechauns roam the lands.*** Many strange creatures roam the green fields of Ireland, (my uncle Tommy being one of them) but leprechauns, I'm

afraid, are not running around the place shouting “bejasus!”

- ***The Irish are always friendly!*** It is true that most Irish people will give you the shirts off their back, there are however a few who wouldn’t give you the steam off their piss.
- ***The Irish are great storytellers.*** Yes, it’s true that many a seanachai entertained our ancestors with stories of heroic tales but the seanachai are a dying breed. The stories told nowadays would bore the balls of a donkey.
- ***The Irish are poor misfortunate mostly rural peasants.*** Now no one is quite sure where this vicious rumour started but we have blamed the English for centuries so I won’t break tradition. This is a complete myth for the

majority of the country, except for the following areas, Leitrim, Longford, and Donegal. These areas are still mostly inhabited by poor, filthy, rural peasants. I'm just kidding (mostly).

- ***The sound of a Banshee (ghost) can be heard throughout the land at night.*** No! What you're more than likely hearing is my uncle, Tommy roaring while roaming the fields. He does be gas that fella!
- ***The Irish are always drunk.*** It's true that the majority of Irish folk are partial to an odd brandy, whiskey, pint, etc., and we head out on the weekends to get locked (drunk) but unlike the British we can actually take our drink.
- ***We only eat potatoes.*** While this was indeed true for centuries, the Great

Famine forced us as a nation to become partial to different types of food. We are now a very sophisticated nation with a varied diet including, steak, Starbucks, pot noodle and lasagne to name but a few

- ***Irish people are all farmers***. This is a major myth just 7.7% of the population are full-time farmers (Census 2010).
- ***It's all cows and green fields***. A lot of the country is taken up with cows and fields but finding either of these in Dublin would be the equivalent of finding a polar bear in the Sahara Desert.
- ***Everyone lives in a thatched roof cottage***. This rumour seemed to go viral (or whatever the equivalent was in the old days) due to popular films

such as “Ryan’s daughter” and “The field.” So no! In fact, there are less than 1,500 thatched roof dwelling in Ireland.

- ***We always wear green, white and gold***. While a lot of the nation dress up on national occasions and for national sport events, my advice is if you see any Irishman dressed in these colours when there are no special national events, well then, you would be best to walk across the street to avoid him.
- ***Irish people are ugly***. Now the Irish were never a nation known for their national beauty but due to a greater widening of the genetic pool things have been improving. Examples, Colin Farrell, Jamie Dornan, Patrick Dempsey and let’s not forget the

ladies, Nadia Forde, Saoirse Ronan, Roseanna Davison. See! All feckin gorgeous!

- ***We wear Kilts and play the bag pipes.*** This is true in Scotland NOT Ireland. If I had a euro for every time I heard a tourist make this mistake, well then I wouldn't have to write this book because I'd be stinking rich.
- ***There is an on-going civil war making a visit to Northern Ireland dangerous!*** I'm shocked at how often I hear this one. While it's true there is still some dissident trouble in the North this is limited to very small and isolated events.
- ***The Islands of Ireland and the United Kingdom are the same***. No, they are not. Ireland is a completely separate

Island with its own government. However, the UK does still own these six northern counties: Antrim, Armagh, Down, Fermanagh, Londonderry, and Tyrone. Confused? Me too!

- ***<u>Irish people only listen to diddle eye music and rebel songs</u>***. False, thanks to MTV and top of the pops we have broadened our horizons musically at least. Most are still partial to some diddle eye music, especially in the Pub.

REAL Irish Facts

Okay so now that's the horse-shit out of the way! Time to get down to the nitty-gritty (details) of what qualities real Irish people possess.

- Irish folk are genetically incapable of keeping a secret.
- We are religious but rarely go to mass.
- Irish people apologise for everything even when they're not in the wrong.
- Irish people generally hate Patricks day. Flocking to the pubs, they drink all day whilst hiding from the yanks outside enjoying the parade usually screaming from their lungs "Oh my God, I'm like sooo Irish" no love, no you're not.

- We become strangely poetic after a few pints.
- Listening is not our strong point. We can't wait for the other person to stop talking so we can start talking instead.
- We love our mammies because they make us Irish stew, tea and fill our hot water bottles.
- Irish stew is really just a euphemism for "boiled leftovers from the fridge."
- Everyone is, or knows, at least one Murphy.
- That reminds me, Murphy 's Law: Anything that can go wrong will go wrong!
- The average height of an Irish man is 5 ft 8 inches.
- The longest place name in Ireland is called Muckanaghederdauhaulia in

County Galway, I hear tis only beautiful.

- We like the odd drink: Irish people consume on average 131.1 litres of beer per year, impressive eh?
- There are more Irish people living outside Ireland than Inside: Yep we do like to spread out wings. 70 million people worldwide claim to have Irish heritage. Including Obama.
- In fact, the white house was designed by an Irish man. Yes, James Hoban won a competition in 1792 allowing him to create the building.
- Ireland's highest mountain is Carraunttoohill, standing at 1041meters.
- Irelands oldest pub is Sean's bar which opened in Athlone in 900AD.

- Irish people love their tea. The average Irish person goes through about 1184 cups each year!
- The Population of Ireland is 4.5 million (2013).
- Irish people talk incessantly about the weather, it's a national hobby.
- Northside/southside: In most Irish cities or towns there is a divide, usually physically by a river. Northsiders are generally thought of as working class folk who embrace the rougher side of life. Southsiders, on the other hand, are more well-to-do (posh) and embrace an even rougher side of life. Sure we're all just big Irish edjets anyway!

- We all drop everything (literally, babies and all) the minute we hear the Angelus.
- The remains of Saint Valentine (the patron saint of love) are buried under a church in Dublin.
- The three most popular boy's names (2015) are Conor, Sean, and Jack.
- The three most popular girl's names (2015) are Emma, Sophie, and Aoife.
- Ambran na bhFiann is the Irish national anthem, but few actually know the words to it!
- The unofficial national anthem is Mark McCabes "Maniac 2000". It was so popular worldwide it even featured in an episode of the Simpson's.
- Saint Patrick wasn't even Irish; he was from Wales. See, us Irish are a very

welcoming bunch, we took in foreigners before we even knew what a foreigner was!

- The Irish flag (green, white and orange) has a specific meaning. The green represents Gaelic Irish, the orange represents Ulster and the white part represents the bit in the middle where the two traditions can co-exist.
- Ireland is the only country in the world whose national symbol is a musical instrument, the harp!
- Getting "the birthday bumps" was a traumatic part of every Irish person childhood. If your schoolmates found out it was your birthday, they would grab you by the hands and feet and proceed to subject you to a succession of lifts and drops, usually over hard

concrete (this depended on their mood). Eventually, there was always one cowardly bastard scared of repercussions and ended the fiasco.

- There are more mobile phones in Ireland than there are people. Sure, we love the auld chit chat.
- The home of Guinness is in Dublin. The famous Guinness Brewery at St. James Gate has a 9,000-year lease. So fear not there are plenty of pints for the foreseeable future.
- Speaking of Guinness, in 1974 a bizarre medical case occurred when a baby was born with the cap of a Guinness stout bottle stuck in its scalp. The only explanation doctors had was that the mother must have accidentally

swallowed the cap at some point in during the pregnancy, lovely!

- An old name for Wicklow people was "goat suckers." Enough said!
- In 1800 the population of Ireland was twice as large as the population of the United States, then the famine happened and fecked it all up for us.
- Ireland is home to the world's longest-running television show. Yep "The Late Late Show" has been running since 1961, discussing controversial issues such as condoms, gay marriage and interviewing the odd Z-list celebrity.

Personality Traits

Yes, we Irish are indeed a quite unique race. Our personality traits differ quite substantially from those of any other civilised—or not so civilised—country. If you really want to be Irish, below is a list of traits that you really should start practicing.

Self-depreciation

Also known as the act of belittling, degrading or undervaluing oneself, usually in the presence of others, in an attempt to appear modest or foolish. This can be a hard trait to grasp if you're not born and bred in Ireland. Especially for the yanks, Christ ye will find this one very difficult. Basically, just tell yourself you're a useless, fat, good for nothing pile of shite for a few days and that will help get you into the mind-set of self-depreciation. Here is an example to make things a bit easier:

Example 1

Woman number 1: *"Mary that's a lovely dress you're wearing."*

Woman number 2: *"Are you serious? It's horrible, I just threw it on 'cause I had nothing else to wear. I look like a pig in it."*

Example 2

Man number 1: *"Paddy you're lookin well."*

Man number 2 *"Well? Are you feckin blind Tommy, I look like a walking corpse, in fact, a corpse would look better than me!"*

You see the key is to NEVER take a compliment, from anyone, EVER!

Embarrassment

This is a pretty basic trait. If an American person gets embarrassed, they will confidently yell “Oh my Gosh I am so embarrassed”. If an Irish person said that, they would die there and then on the spot. When an Irish person gets embarrassed, firstly, they hope nobody has noticed the embarrassing incident. Then they get paranoid, their face turns a peculiar purple colour, beads of sweat appear on their forehead and the final step is to cower for cover in a corner praying to the good Lord above that the ground will open up and swallow you whole. (It rarely does.)

Example: Pretend somebody has tripped in a busy street.

The American: *"Oh my gosh, Oh Gosh I am soooo embarrassed, excuse me, excuse me Sir could you help me up please, why thank you soooo much."*

The Irish: They say nothing, why? Because they jumped back up faster than they fell down and ran down the street with a big purple head on them.

So the key is to NEVER draw unwanted attention to yourself, EVER!

Black Humour

Everyone knows what humour is right? Well, let's just say the Irish have a peculiar take on it. Black Irish humour basically refers to making sick, hurtful, morally wrong jokes at the most desperate of times in a rather futile attempt to lighten the mood. Nobody is quite sure when this came info fashion but the educated guess would suggest somewhere in or around 1845. The great famine was happening at this time and we were feckin starving and miserable because the Brits stole the last few decent potatoes we had left. Anyway we Irish are not ones to hold a grudge.

If you really want to be Irish, you need to incorporate some black humour into those sad, terrible times we all go through at one point or another.

> Example 1: Mary is in bed dying, she has only hours to live.

Woman: *"Aren't you the lucky one Mary, getting out of this shithole."*

Mary: *"Sure I'm looking forward to it, better than listening to ye lot any day."*

Example 2: Paddy loses his right arm in a farming accident.

Man 1 "*I heard you were fighting with the tractor again Paddy."*

Paddy *"Oh Christ, I was, Mick, but the bastard won this time."*

So as you can see, never take a serious situation seriously, Ever!

Banter

Aah, banter, the greatest thing since the sliced pan. Banter has been around for centuries. It refers to the exchange of often insulting humiliating remarks in a good-humoured teasing way. Now banter can be found in many cultures throughout the world but the Irish banter is slightly cruder, slightly more insulting and slightly more politically incorrect. Us Irish don't like to do things by half measures.

> Example 1: Two men who are lifelong friends engage in some friendly banter.
>
> Man 1: *"You're nothing but an auld (old) bastard Paddy!"*
>
> Man 2: *"Right back at ya Tommy, ya ignorant pile of shite!"*
>
> Example 2: Two co-workers are working in an office.
>
> Woman 1: *"I hate my job!"*

Woman 2: *"Do you know there's a support group for that?"*

Woman 1: *"Really?"*

Woman 2: *"Yea it's called EVERYONE, they meet in the pub on a Friday night."*

So NEVER give anyone an inch, 'cause they'll take a feckin mile!

Hypocrite (Two-faced!)

Tis' true, us Irish are a bunch of feckin hypocrites and we're proud of it. The Argentinian novelist Maria Araoz summed it up quite well when she said: "If there were only three Irish men in the world you'd find two of them in the corner talking about the other!" It's not something we do out of badness, it's more like a subconscious hobby that passes the time.

Example: Three men are working in on a building site laying concrete blocks.

Man 1: *"You're a great little worker Sean, isn't he Paddy?"*

Man 2: *"Oh Christ John he is, a great little worker our Sean."*

Man 3: *"Thanks, lads, I'm just goin to the jacks (toilet) I'll be back in two minutes."*

One minute later

Man 1: *"He's a lazy fuckin bastard that Sean."*

Man 2 *"Oh he is, wouldn't do a stroke (thing) the lazy shite."*

So NEVER talk bad about anyone, until they turn their back on you!

Bligard/Bluffer/Faker

The art of being a bligard is something built into all Irish men from birth. It’s a tricky one to describe. Basically it's similar to a poker bluff, you big yourself up in the hope that some feckin edjet actually thinks you have a good hand, which you don’t.

> Example: A group of men are talking at work on a Monday morning:
>
> Man 1: *“Good weekend lads?”*
>
> Man 2: *“I did anyway, I drank twenty pints Saturday night and had another ten for breakfast the following morning.”*

Man 3: *"You're an awful edjet!"*

As you can tell man number two was bligarding/bluffing or just being a gobshite!

So, NEVER underestimate yourself, instead overestimate and exaggerate everything!

Restraint/unemotional

The Irish don't like to get too excited, happy or enthusiastic about anything. If you ask an Irish person how they are feeling the answer will be "I'm grand! Now feck off!". We don't like making a fuss and we certainly don't like letting anyone know we are feeling bad or good for that matter. It's as if we are stuck in limbo all the time, neither happy nor sad, hence the term "I'm grand." W.B Yeats put it very well when he said: "Being Irish, he had an abiding sense of tragedy, which sustained him through temporary periods of joy." It's as if we are afraid to get too happy because we know some gobshite will come along and feckin ruin it.

> Example 1: A woman bumps into her neighbour while doing the messages (groceries):
>
> Woman 1: "How are ye Mary?"
>
> Woman 2: "I'm grand and yourself?"
>
> Woman 1: "Grand? But sure wasn't your house only get burnt to the ground last night, you're lucky to be alive."
>
> Woman 2: "Aaa don't be so dramatic, sure I'm grand!"

Example 2: Two men are in a pub while the lottery is on

Man 1: “Bejasus I’m only after winning the feckin lotto Paddy.”

Man 2: “You’re jokin?”

Man 1: “Why would I be jokin?”

Man 2: “Are you excited?”

Man 1: “Year sure, I’m grand,”

So NEVER, show extreme happiness or sadness, EVER!

Religion

If you want to be Irish, then religion is very important. Now most Irish people are unsure what religion they are but they know they're religious all the same. Nobody in Ireland really gives a shite what religion you are, once you don't start harping (talking) on about it incessantly. There's nothing worse than listening to a pieus holy joe.

A pieus holy joe*: An edjet who is very religious and thinks the sun shines out of their backside because they go to mass every Sunday. They look down their nose at irregular mass goers and spend their free time polishing their halo. These fascinating creatures are found in every parish throughout Ireland. If you're still unsure, attend a mass in any church and they can be found dishing out the Holy Communion mid-way through the service.*

Apparitions

There is nothing us Irish love more than a good old-fashioned apparition, in fact, they are one of our favourite pastimes. Over the years, there have been many, many reports of apparitions. An apparition is when holy God, Mary, Jesus or sometimes Joseph appears out of nowhere to say hello. They can happen anywhere and are usually unexpected. The two most well-known apparitions took place in Knock and Ballinadee.

Knock: One wet miserable evening on August 21, 1879 the inhabitants of the small village of Knock in County Mayo were going about their day to day business doing the messages (groceries), milking the cows and the likes. Anyway, didn't the holy Mary only decide to appear to the villagers and scare the bejasus out of them. Not only that wasn't she joined by Saint Joseph and Saint John also. After getting over the fright of it, they decided they had better do their moral duty and say a few decades of the rosary, seeing as Mary, Joseph and John had come so far to see them. After a while, it started to lash rain so the visitors returned to heaven leaving the locals the task of telling the world what they had seen.

So fast forward 137 years and Knock is a mecca for religious tourists coming from around the world to pray in the church. The main strip is quite similar to the main strip of Las Vegas. Bright lights, tacky souvenir shops and even tackier tourists line the streets. A great day out for all the family.

Ballinspittle: In 1985 a fella was driving along the road in the small village of Ballinspittle County Cork and what happened only didn't the village statue of holy Mary start dancing around the place. Thinking he was going mad, he made his way to the doctor's office to tell him about the situation. To his surprise, the doctor looked out the window and said: "Bejasus Tommy you're right, the feckin thing is moving." Within hours, the entire village had gathered to watch the statue of holy Mary moving all around the place. The media got whiff of this and within days, crowds flocked from all over the country to see Mary and her newfound dance moves. Over 100,000 people made their way to Ballinspittle to see the statue. My father and uncle being amongst the crowd. I consider my father and uncle to be sane men of able mind and body. To this day they both say that they clearly saw the statue moving, in fact, they stayed there for hours looking at it in disbelief. So you can make up your own mind but that's the story of Ballinspittle and the moving statue.

If you want to see the statue today, it sits about a mile along the Ballinspittle to Kinsale road. It's a blue grotto and the statue is about four metres above road level, Sure, you can't miss it!

Religious occasions

There are many religious occasions in the Irish social calendar. Here we go through a small few and discuss the true meaning behind them.

Christenings: There's nothing more precious than a newborn baby. So when the baby is just a few weeks old, we bring it to the church to be christened. This consists of standing at the altar with your respective partner and the (usually) roaring baby. The priest says a few words and then pours cold holy water over its head, the baby is by now in convulsions crying, the parents start bickering on the altar and everyone pretends to smile for a few photos.

Afterwards, the mother in law or a kind neighbour minds the baby while everyone else heads to the pub to get locked (drunk)!

Holy Communions: This is a very lucrative day for any child. Everyone heads to the church dressed in fancy clothes, a white dress for the girls and usually a uniform or something smart for the boys. They kids are about ten years of age and commit themselves to Christ. From that day fourth they are allowed receive the body of Christ in mass, in other words, they get to eat the tiny free piece of bread handed out by the pieus holy joes we mentioned earlier.

Then after the church, it's time for photos. All the relatives and neighbours of the family give the child a card with cash inside. The afternoon is usually spent chasing the odd mean fecker who thought he was going to be a cute whore (smartass) and get away without giving the poor child a euro. Once all the money has been extorted its straight to the pub. The kids obviously drink a soft drink or occasionally a brandy. That's a joke (mostly).

Confirmation: (See Holy Communion) This occasion is similar to the holy communion but the children are slightly older by now, generally twelve, and so have greater interest/value in the money. After a gruelling three-hour ceremony, everyone is feckin starving so it's straight to a restaurant for some fancy food. Then down to the pub where everyone has a drink and I mean everyone!

Weddings: The Irish wedding is another religious occasion. Two (usually) happy people come together in church to profess their love for each other in front of holy God, the priest, the pieus holy joes, and many family and friends. The bride wears a lovely geansai (dress) and the man wears his old school uniform if it still fits him and if not then he reluctantly invests in a suit. They stand at the altar, profess their faith and love and when the priest gives the go-ahead they give each other a big smooch (kiss) and pretend like they've done nothing else because they were waiting for the wedding night.

The photographer takes some photos out in the pissing rain and everyone looks like a drowned rat. Afterwards, it's on to the wedding venue which is usually the fanciest hotel in town. Guests must hand over an envelope containing cash as a gift to gain entrance. This is a somewhat new phenomenon, up until the Celtic Tiger it was quite acceptable to buy a normal gift like a toaster or a kettle but nowadays nothing less than €200 will suffice. This recent change has caused a decline in the number of guests at a wedding, causing some couples to be forced to rent a crowd for the big day. If you're invited to a wedding and you dislike or don't give a shite about the bride or groom, then you make up a sneaky excuse so that you can hold onto the €200 quid.

Everyone drinks and gets drunk until the early hours of the following morning. There are very few marriages in Ireland consecrated on the actual wedding night. By the time the bride and groom get back to their hotel room, their heads do be spinning from all the drink, they climb into bed, the room starts to spin and they get sick. Lovely! So that's the Irish wedding, tis great craic!

Funerals/wakes: Funerals in Ireland are basically big parties. People celebrate the deceased person's life, or if they disliked the deceased person, they party because they "never liked the fecker in the first place." The Mass part is fairly sad alright, the priest says a few kind words about the deceased, and even the most awful bastard gets a few kind words. The coffin is shouldered out of the church into the hearse and on to the graveyard. Unable or unwilling to express any type of emotion, we bottle it all up until we get to the pub. Then we start downing pints as if there is no tomorrow until we are so locked nobody will remember if we have a moment of weakness and start crying or talking about how sad the entire thing is.

The Irish funeral is also the only occasion you will run into all those second, third and god knows how many other many generations of cousins you have.

The Weather

Now if you want to be Irish, you need to become obsessed with the weather. Yes, that's right you heard me, obsessed! In fact, a major food retailer carried out a study in 2012 asking Irish people what they thought about most often? The answer was, that's right you guessed it, the weather! Now remember this was 2012, the country was still in the middle of a fiscal crisis, unemployment was rampant and there was also a severe housing crisis, but all we could think about was the weather, sure aren't we gas!

There are many reasons the Irish are so intrigued by the weather. I guess the first thing to remember is that Ireland is one of the few countries in the world that literally gets four seasons in one day. It could be snowing in the morning, raining at midday, sunny in the afternoon and hurricane Charlie (he's an awful fecker) could strike without warning that night. See, four seasons in one fecking day, tis' desperate!

The main thing to remember is that it rains a lot in Ireland, and I really do mean a lot. The strange thing is us Irish are in complete denial about this. We never have an umbrella or raincoat with us, it's as if we have convinced ourselves on some subconscious level that we live in the sunny Caribbean and rain is a rare occurrence. So when it starts "pissing outa the heavens" we stand there, soaked to the skin, without any rain gear and say: "Jasus that shower came out of nowhere!"

On the plus side of things, we love summer, because it rains less? No, not quite but because the rain is a bit feckin warmer!

The weather is also the focal point of almost all random conversations amongst Irish people. It's not so much that we care about the weather it's just an easy ever changing topic to talk about in awkward situations. For example, if you were buying bread in the supermarket and bumped into an old boss who you slept with, you would just say, "Isn't the weather awful Martin." Instead of cowering in the corner in shame. See, the weather is literally the answer to every awkward encounter.

Now if you are going to be truly Irish you will need to know the lingo (terminology) used when talking or thinking about the weather so here we go:

- **There's a grand auld stretch in the evenings!** After Christmas, the evenings become longer due to the change of GMT time. This is a slow process because Irish people have a knack for noticing even the most minute stretch in the days, (even as little as 5 seconds). The phenomenon of "the grand stretch" will dominate all social interactions until June.
- **The dark evenings are really starting to creep in!** When summer GMT time comes to an end in June, the evenings begin to become gradually darker. This phenomenon dominates all social interactions until December. Tis a vicious cycle!
- **There's great drying out!** This is a favourite with Irish mammies across the isle of Ireland. They derive great pleasure from smugly informing their nearest and dearest of the great drying

magical properties that are present in their back garden!

- **It's absolutely bitter out there!** When there is a notable decrease in air temperature, Irish people hobble around, rubbing their hands together saying, "tis absolutely BIT-THURRR out there!
- **Sure the weather is desperate!** This is used quite commonly when the weather (or the speaker) is unstable (mentally).
- **You wouldn't put the dog out in it!** This one is pretty self-explanatory. When the weather is pure shite and you wouldn't even but your beloved mongrel out in it tis so bad.
- **It's awful warm!** Irish people are used to miserable, wet, windy weather. When we get the odd increase in temperature we generally find it hard to cope and have no idea what to do with it, so we just sit around and complain saying, "tis WAR-HUM"
- **Is it raining?** This is a very common term used throughout the country. Example: you arrive home after being

down to the shops and are clearly soaked to the skin. Usually, your Dad will ask sarcastically, "Is it raining?"

- **It's going to get worse before it gets better!** Aaah yes, the Irish, eternal optimists. This is used when describing how awful the weather is and how bad it will be over the coming days. Now remember in Ireland we generally don't get tornados, tropical storms or heatwaves so really we are complaining about nothing. Sure tis just something to talk about really!
- **Tis going to freeze like a bitch!** If its cold outside and there's a clear sky, every single Irish person starts talking about the frost and telling their nearest and dearest to watch out for it on the roads.
- **Do you remember the big freeze?** This phrase is used when referring to "the big freeze" of 2010. This was one of the worst events in Irish history since the great famine. The country came to a standstill as the worst winter in living memory wreaked havoc across the

country. We love reminiscing about it thought as t'was the most exciting thing that happened since, well, since the famine!

- **I wonder what the weather is like back home?** We say this when we are abroad, usually in Spain and the sun is batting down on us. Secretly we wish we were back in miserable, wet, windy Ireland as our bodies find it hard to cope with the tropical Spanish temperatures.
- **The heat is cruel!** Used during holidays in warm sunny climates and or at home during the odd hot summers day, which we generally find excruciating!

Heroes

If you are serious about being Irish, then you will need to educate yourself about some of its heroes. Ireland has had many a hero throughout the centuries, here I will pick my favourite three (and in my opinion the most popular) and give you all the gory details.

Cuchulainn (*Pronounced Cu-cul-an)*

This fella was as tough as auld boots! Basically, he was a mythical Irish warrior and the champion of Ulster. He was undefeatable in battle and the most prominent hero of Ulster.

Legend has it he was born at Newgrange (well worth a visit). He was a pure mad bastard and single-handedly fought the armies of Queen Mebh of Connacht. Now didn't the wicked Queen Mebh only put the armies of Ulster to sleep with her hocus pocus, leaving poor auld Cuchulainn to defend Ulster's lands all on his tod (his own).

The story goes that he fought off the Queen's armies one man at a time in a combat that lasted months. He must have been feckin exhausted! Anyway, this is not a happy ending as eventually Queen Mebh contrived with his enemies to bring him to battle. She put a spell on him and he was wounded by a spear thrown by some fecker named Lugaid (sure with a name like that he would have to be a right gobshite). Being the cute whore (smart fella) he was, didn't Cuchulainn tie himself standing upright to a rock so that his enemies would think he was unhurt. But sure didn't a crow land on his shoulder and start pecking away at the poor devil and the enemies returned to kill him. But not before Cuchulainn killed Lugaid with the last bit of energy he had. A mighty man if there was ever one!

Fionn McCumhail (Pronounced Fi-un Mac-Cool)

This fella had an eventful life to say the least. When he was a boy, he worked as a servant for a local wealthy poet. The poet spent seven years fishing for a funny fish called the "salmon of knowledge". This salmon, legend has it, had all the knowledge of the world inside it and whoever caught and ate the fish would gain this knowledge. The poet eventually caught the fish and gave Fionn the task of cooking the salmon, warning him not to dare eat it. But sure while cooking it didn't poor little Fionn burn his finger on the fish fat and put it straight into his mouth to try and ease the pain. Little did he know that this was enough to transfer the knowledge. His eyes lit up like something out of a horror movie and he was now the smartest person on the island of Ireland.

With his new found intelligence, he grew up to be the leader of a right rough gang of Irish warriors known as the Fianna. While out hunting one day, he saw the most beautiful deer he had ever seen. So instead of killing it he decided to take it home. Sure what happened when he got home? Didn't the deer turn into a gorgeous woman who later became his wife. They had a son called Oisin and lived happily ever after, well almost!

You see Fionn was scared of nobody and loved being the big man and getting into fights. So legend has it he got up on morning rearing for an argument. His arch enemy was a Scottish giant called Benandonner. Legend has it that Fionn built "Giants causeway" in

Country Antrim to get to Scotland to battle it out with Benandonner. When he got there, however, things didn't go according to plan. Benandonner was asleep when Fionn arrived. It was Fionn's first time laying eyes on Benandonner and he was fecking massive, in fact almost three times the size of Fionn. Being a fast thinking knowledgeable Irish man, he fled the scene and returned home to his wife.

Now, some sneaky fecker told Benandonner that Fionn had fled and Benandonner, enraged, ran across the causeway to find Fionn. As they heard the loud footsteps and roaring of the giant, Fionn and his wife began to panic. But being the most knowledgeable man in Ireland, he knew what to do. He told his wife to dress him up as a baby, yep that's right, a baby! When Benandonner arrived, he took one look at the "baby". Fionn's wife told the giant that is was Fionn's son. The Scottish giant pondered for a while and thought, *If this is the size of Fionn's baby then I would hate to see the size of Fionn himself!* So, scared out of his wits, the Scottish giant ran back home and never bothered Fionn again. Now some may say Fionn was a coward but you have to admit t'was a smart thing to do!

Conor McGregor aka The Notorious

Now this fella is a more recent hero of Ireland. Unknown to most until just a few years ago, he has been catapulted into fame for his world-renowned fighting skills and is now a household name. There is no doubt that McGregor is a man of skill after spending years honing his skills. Starting boxing at the age of sixteen, he soon became interested in MMA. He was signed to the UFC in February 2013 and, well, the rest is history.

Besides his obvious legendary fighting ability, there are a few other reasons why the Irish are so obsessed with McGregor. Sure we like to see one of our own doing well, plus he is the essence of Irishness. He talks the talk and he can certainly walk the walk. His cocky attitude is as entertaining as watching the fights. Thousands of his countrymen practically take over Las Vegas during his fights and he apparently is as proud of us as we are of him.

"The whole world is looking at our country; the eyes are on the Irish. I'm proud of that and very, very grateful. I'm extremely proud of my nation."

In my opinion, McGregor symbolises the things that have always and will always be historically Irish: talking and fighting. After making it big, he asked all his family to put their bills on the table, he would take care of them! What a legend! Sorry, Conor I think we are distant cousins and I have a load of bills for that table!

His style is pretty epic for an Irish man, the Louis Copeland suits, the bling, the attitude, most of us Irishmen try our best to emulate his style. We strut around the nightclubs in ill-fitting suits on a Saturday night with our shades on, pretending to be McGregor but sure everyone knows we are only doing da edjet!

Here is my all-time favourite McGregor quote:

"I'd love a monkey, maybe a chimpanzee. Just a cool chimpanzee whipping around, that would be unbelievable."

It certainly would Conor, it certainly would!
Sure isn't he gas!

The GAA

The GAA stands for Gaelic Athletic Association. The association itself was found in 1884 but the games themselves have been played for centuries. The most common games are football (not to be confused with soccer) and hurling. Football is where a load of fellas run around a field chasing a ball but they can use their hands, unlike soccer. Hurling is where a load of fellas run around a pitch with a big stick and try to hit a small piece of round leather (sliotair) into the goal. Sounds like fun right? Well, I must admit tis' great craic altogether. So if you want to be Irish, then you had better get involved in the GAA.

Now of course, you may not necessarily be willing to run around the pitch chasing a ball but that's no excuse, almost everyone in Ireland is involved in the GAA in one form or another. So if you can't be a player, you can at least watch the televised games or make the sandwiches for your local team or scrub the floor in the local GAA hall. See, there's always something to be done! So go on, don't be shy, just get stuck in.

Oh and just because you don't live in Ireland, that's no excuse. Thousands of people of Irish diaspora play GAA in countries outside of Ireland. Sure even the United States marines have a hurling team! Below are some more weird and wacky facts about the GAA.

- In 1845, people were banned from playing hurling in Quebec City as it was considered too dangerous!
- Over 8,000 people in mainland Europe play GAA games!
- In Milwaukee they have a thing called "Hurloween" where they dress up in Halloween costumes and play hurling, aren't they gas feckers!
- GAA players don't get paid a cent! So the player playing on national TV in front of a screaming nation on a Sunday will be back selling bacon on Monday.
- In hurling, the ball can hit speeds in excess of 100 mph.
- Many claim that Ice hockey originated from hurling.

- Croke Park is where major matches and finals are held. People go up to Dublin for the big day out. We get locked if our team wins and we get locked if they lose so tis a win-win situation really!
- Croke Park is one of the top five stadiums in Europe, sure aren't we fancy out eh!
- Cork is good at hurling.
- Kerry is good at football.
- Then you have the likes of poor auld Leitrim who are shite at both!
- Over 350,000 Hurleys (the sticks they use to bate the sliotair/ball) are made in Ireland every year! Pretty impressive considering the population of Ireland is only about 4.5 million.

The Pub

Irish pubs have existed for well over a millennium. So basically, the Irish have been drinking for centuries! There are an estimated 7,000 Irish themed pubs worldwide so you have no excuse; no matter where you live, there is probably an Irish pub just around the corner!

The pub has been a pillar of the Irish community for centuries. It's the only place you get to see all your neighbours and hear all the local and non-local gossip. Everyone is generally friendly and welcoming in Irish pubs so you have no excuses! The best thing about Irish pubs, in my opinion, is when you head down for a "quiet one" and you wake up the following morning in a ditch with a traffic cone stuck to your head, aah the happy memories!

Now beware that we Irish take drinking and pub etiquette seriously. Below are some guidelines to keep you on the straight and narrow!

- Never disturb the old men sitting quietly at the bar, they've had a hard auld life and are riddled with arthritis from head to toe!
- Buy a round, nobody likes a cheap skate and trust me it won't go unnoticed!
- Share your taytos, there's nothing worse than a mean tight fisted bastard who won't give ya a tayto, trust me they are out there!
- Don't be the gobshite who is shit-faced and falling into everyone, nobody likes that guy, nobody!
- Don't be afraid to talk, and don't whisper either. Sure tis all about the craic!
- Never start drinking your pint of Guinness before it has fully settled! You would be wise to remember this one if you want to avoid unwanted attention.
- Telling lies is unacceptable. However, you may grossly exaggerate any or all of your stories!

- Never, ever wave to get the barman's attention, trust me he sees you and will serve you in due course.
- If you see a hottie and decide to hit on her just remember, chances are, her father, brothers and uncles are among the crowd waiting to pounce!
- Found a new friend, then by them a drink! Buying an Irish person a drink is the equivalent to handing them €100.
- If you get confused to which pint is yours, just grab the fullest one!
- Never try to leave whilst in the midst of a lock-in! Never! (A lock-in is when everyone is still drinking in the pub after legal hours, tis mighty craic!)

The Language

Language in Ireland is a complicated matter. As mentioned earlier in the book, few people speak Irish on a daily basis. However, most of us use a few words here and there just to aggravate the foreigners if no more. Also, the chances are if you're traveling to the west or to Leitrim you will be likely to come across a stubborn fecker who will refuse to use anything but his beloved Gaeilge. So below I have listed some words and phrases to help you in case you get stuck!

Dia dhuit *Hello* (DEE-a-Gwit)

Conas ata tu? *How are you?* (Cunn-us-a-TAW too?)

Taim go maith *I'm good!* (Taw-im guh Mah)

Cad is ainm duit? *What is your name?* (COD-iss Annim dit?)

Sean is ainm dom *Sean is my name* (Sean iss annim dum)

Deas ag bualadh leat *Nice to meet you* (Jahss egg Boo-loo lyaht)

Go ndeanai mhaith duit/daoibh *You're welcome* (Goh nyae-nee why dit)

Le do thoil *Please* (Le do Hull)

Go raibh maith agat *Thank you* (Gud rave mah ag-ut)

Ni hea *No* (Nee ha)

Ta bro norm *I'm sorry* (Taw brohn ur-im)

Slan *Goodbye* (Slawn)

Nil aon Gaeilge agam *I can't speak Irish* (Neel aon Gwayl-ag-a agum)

Any bhfuil Bearla agat? *Do you speak Irish?* (An will Bay-er-la ag-ut?)

Foir Dom! *Help!* (Fore dum!)

Maidin maith *Good morning* (May-jin mah)

Trathnona maith *Good evening* (Trah-no-nuh mah)

Oiche mhaith *Good night* (EE-ha-mah)

Ca bhfuil an leithreas? *Where is the toilet?* (Caw will an leh-her-as?)

Ni thuigim *I don't understand* (Nee Higg-im)

Teach tabhairne *Pub* (Tea-ach tower-na)

An deidir leat cabhru liom amach as an dio le do thoil?

Can you help me get out of this ditch, please?

(Un feadar lat cabru lum amack ass un diug le du hul)

Slang Terminology/Phrases

1.	**Sham**	A friend
2.	**Gowl**	Annoyingly stupid person
3.	**Feek**	Gorgeous girl
4.	**Quare**	Another word for unusual
5.	**Yoke**	Thing
6.	**Savage**	Can be good or bad
7.	**Pure**	Really/very
8.	**Cat**	An effusive way to say it is awful or terrible
9.	**Sound**	Reliable, dependable, person
10.	**Tool**	Idiot
11.	**Shades**	Garda Siochana (Police)

12.	**Muppet**	Fool
13.	**Banjaxed**	Broken
14.	**Fierce**	Very
15.	**Shift**	French kiss
16.	**Gammy**	Useless
17.	**Manky**	Very soiled/smelly
18.	**Deadly**	Fantastic
19.	**Ride**	A good-looking person
20.	**Bullin**	Angry
21.	**Gimp**	Fool or idiot.
22.	**Flute**	A bit of a silly person
23.	**Narky**	Cranky
24.	**Class**	A term used for something good
25.	**Wan**	One or woman
26.	**Plastered**	To be very drunk
27.	**Bogger**	Rural person
28.	**Hames**	To ruin or destroy
29.	**Whist**	Be quiet

30.	**Meet**	To French kiss
31.	**Rotten**	Something horrible or disgusting
32.	**Mouldy**	To get drunk
33.	**Ossified**	Drunk
34.	**Feen**	Male
35.	**Grand**	Fine, OK, alright
36.	**Stall**	Stop
37.	**Bate**	Exhausted
38.	**Sup**	Hello
39.	**Gander**	A look
40.	**Scuttered**	In a very advanced state of intoxication
41.	**Well**	How are you?
42.	**Slash**	Urinating
43.	**Gaff**	House
44.	**Beour**	Female
45.	**Scoops**	Alcoholic drink
46.	**Sketch**	Used when keeping

		a lookout for an authority figure
47.	**Horse**	A friend
48.	**Aye**	Yes
49.	**Clatter**	A slap or a belt
50.	**Score**	To kiss someone
51.	**Bure**	Female
52.	**Buck**	Boy, man, lad
53.	**Wide**	Aware of, understand
54.	**Gawk**	Sick
55.	**Scatter**	A group
56.	**Puss**	Sulky face
57.	**Amadan**	Fool
58.	**Spanner**	An idiot
59.	**Jackeen**	Person from Dublin
60.	**Clem**	Something bad
61.	**Chancer**	Dodgy character
62.	**Gom**	Fool
63.	**Bóg**	Illegal dancing pill

		or bomb
64.	**Hape**	Loads
65.	**Hi**	No meaning, used a lot!
66.	**Cop On**	Get over yourself
67.	**Baytin**	Regional pronunciation of the word beating.
68.	**Coddin**	Joking
69.	**Acting The Maggot**	Acting in a particularly foolish manner
70.	**Snake**	Sneaky person
71.	**Gatch**	The walk of someone
72.	**Stall The Ball**	Hold on a moment
73.	**Gombeen**	Fool
74.	**Scratcher**	Bed
75.	**Arseways**	To make a mess of
76.	**Jammy**	Lucky person
77.	**Gas**	Funny

78.	**Jacks**	Toilet
79.	**Craic**	Fun, banter
80.	**Dose**	That's annoying
81.	**Mitch**	To bunk off
82.	**Skank**	Woman of ill repute
83.	**Slag**	A woman of ill repute
84.	**Stocious**	To be very drunk
85.	**Puck**	To hit with a closed fist
86.	**Wee**	Small
87.	**Massive**	Great, super
88.	**Buckled**	Under the influence
89.	**Gobshite**	Someone who annoys you
90.	**Schkelp**	To thump/hit
91.	**Pandy**	Cork speak for mashed spuds, milk and butter

92.	**Cut**	The state of
93.	**Yokes**	Ecstasy tablets
94.	**Banter**	Ne craic/fun, etc.
95.	**Scumbag**	A low-life/thug
96.	**Mighty**	Very good
97.	**Rank**	Mouldy
98.	**Scald**	A cup of tea
99.	**Knackered**	Tired
100.	**Edjet**	A version of the word idiot, pronounced edgit

Now that's the top terminology out of the way! Sure you're practically Irish already! Here are the ten most popular Irish slang phrases as voted for on Facebook:

1. **I didn't do naathin** *I done no such thing.*

2. **D'ya know what I mean like?** *Do you comprehend me?*
3. **I will in me fuck** *I most certainly will do no such thing.*
4. **She'd lie down in a bed of nettles** *A lady with a reputation!*
5. **Are ya ragin?** *Are you angry/pissed off/ annoyed?*
6. **You're about as useful as a Kerry man with a hurley** *You're useless!*
7. **C'mere till I tell ya** *Come closer, I want to bitch about somebody we both know.*
8. **Tell me this and tell me no more** *I want detailed information and I want it now!*
9. **I will yea** *I* most certainly will not!
10. **Yera naw!** *Of course.*

Important Places

Now if you want to be truly Irish, then there are a few places you should visit. The places listed below are famous throughout Ireland, many of us were dragged kicking and screaming to these locations on our school holidays, sure tis' all part of being Irish.

The Ring of Kerry: This is a long drive around Kerry that takes in the breath-taking scenery, idyllic small towns and villages, the spectacular lakes and of course the most famous Killarney nation park. The yanks (Americans) love it there and sure why wouldn't they, tis only beautiful to be fair! Whilst there, why not take a small detour to Skellig Michael where part of the Star Wars filming took place! A slice of Hollywood in Kerry.

The Cliffs of Moher: These cliffs show off Ireland's rugged, craggy coastline. Stretching almost 5 miles in length and 702 feet in height the cliffs really do have to be seen to be believed. The view from the cliffs allows you to see the Aran Islands, Galway bay, and the many, many mountains. Over one million people visit the cliffs every year. Just be careful, many a gobshite has been blown off on a windy day!

Giants Causeway: As mentioned in the folklore tales earlier, this is a popular tourist spot located in County Antrim, Northern Ireland. The scientists say it was created by a volcanic eruption 60 million years ago but the Fionn McCumhail myth is a more likely explanation!

Bunratty Castle: The most complete and authentic medieval experience in Ireland, Bunratty County Clare is a must see for all. Built in 1425 it was restored to its former glory in 1954. The castle itself is surrounded by many cottages and a folk park which give an insight into life is Ireland throughout the ages.

TIP: At night time the castle holds impressive medieval banquets, patrons dress up in medieval clothing and all food, music and entertainment is medieval in style, tis great craic and the drink is medieval too!

Newgrange: Located in County Meath, this Neolithic structure is over 5,000 years old. This is an ancient temple consisting of a large circular mound, a stone passageway and numerous chambers inside. It is known worldwide for the illumination of the passages which takes place once a year known as the winter solstice. At dawn on December 19th to 23rd, a narrow bean penetrates the roof, reaches the floor of the chamber and gradually extends to the end of the structure. Pretty impressive considering it was build thousands of years ago. Sure, even our ancestors were great!

Dublin City: Now you can't be Irish if you haven't been to the capital city, Dublin. The city is packed with things to do, from shopping to sightseeing. Open top bus tours are a great way to see the city and stop at all major attractions. While there check out the following, the many pubs and restaurants of Temple bar. Trinity College, Croke Park, the Guinness store house and last but certainly not least, the GPO. Yes, every Irishman has at one point or another been to the GPO

(General Post Office) to see the bullet holes in the walls from the 1916 rebellion!

Galway city: Situated on the western shoreline, Galway is a great base for trips to the Aran Islands and the Cliffs of Moher. The city itself is quaint and quiet. Yet with plenty of pubs and plenty of nearby attractions, it is certainly a city not to be missed!

Cork City: Also known as "the real capital" Cork is a bustling city in the southern part of the country. A friendly bunch they affectionately refer to their loved ones as a "langer". Anyway, moving swiftly along, there are many attractions through the city, from exploring the English market fit for a queen to ringing the Shandon church bells. The city has its own airport and is a great base for exploring idyllic west Cork, the Bearla peninsula, and neighbouring counties.

Do’s and Don’ts for Tourists

Don’t Ask for a “full English breakfast” in the morning at the hotel or B&B you’re staying in because you’ll be thrown out before you can even say “Good morning”.

Don’t Try to mimic the accent.

Don’t talk about leprechauns.

Don’t sing “Danny boy” in the middle of the street/pub/shop, etc.

Don’t describe yourself as 100% pure Irish.

Don’t forget to get your round in.

Don’t expect a mythological Ireland. If you say the word mythological to any Irish person, they will just look confused and start talking about the weather.

Don’t criticise Ireland. Tis alirght for us locals to give out about the state of the nation but we take offence if outsiders do the same, feckin cheek of ye!

Don't drive on the wrong side of the feckin road! (We drive on the left.)

Do have the craic!

Do bring a rain coat and brolley.

Do get shitfaced!

Do use a few words of Gaeilge.

Do get off the beaten track, (Temple bar is not off the beaten track.)

Do talk to randomers. (Sure we love to chat.)

Do visit some or all of the cool places listed in the previous chapter.

The Law

The last thing you want to do on any trip to the great Isle of Ireland is to break the laws of the land. Below are real laws written into legislation. Please be aware that the people of Ireland take these laws quite seriously and any breaking of these laws could result in arrest and/or further prosecution.

- **It is illegal to be drunk in a pub:** Unbelievable but true! Don't worry, the Gardai (police) turn a blind eye to this one!

- **It is illegal to smoke tobacco on Grafton Street, Dublin City.** The ironic thing about this law is that Dublin's two main tobacco shops are located on Grafton Street, only in Ireland sure!

- **If a leprechaun calls at your door you must, by law, give him a share of your dinner.** Sure the poor little fella would be starving from looking for that pot of gold under the rainbow.

- **Holders of the freedom of Dublin have the right to pasture sheep on common ground within the city boundaries.** Bono and The Edge from the band U2 done this a few years ago, feckin edjets!

- **You can drive around on public roads without ever proving your competency at driving.** Now don't be worrying, sure we're great drivers, us Irish.

- **It is illegal to conduct nuclear tests in the city.** See now you can leave your bio-hazard suit at home.

- **It is illegal to perform any form of witchcraft in the city.** My sincere apologies to any witches, harry potter fans, etc.

- **Crossing a railway track on a bicycle is illegal.** Feckin hippies!

- **It is illegal for a student to walk through Trinity College without a sword.** Sadly, this law is rarely executed.

- **The Tippling Act of 1735 prohibits a publican from pursuing a customer for money owed for any drink given on credit.** This is why it is impossible to start a "tab" in the local pub.

- **The penalty for suicide is death by hanging.** This law was changed only recently in 1968!

- **You are legally entitled to demand a glass of port while sitting any exam in Trinity College, Dublin.** Make mine a double!

- **It is illegal to insult anyone's religion in Ireland under the defamation act**

of 2009. Sure tis all the same God anyway, right?

- **The funniest of all laws: You must hold a TV licence for any device capable of receiving TV signals.** Yes, tis true, even if you don't even use the feckin TV or its broken or you just watch DVDs on it!

Turn the page for your free bonus pictures of hot naked Irish men & women!

Fooled ye! There are none! Dirty perverts! What would your mammies say? Now go on away off and say a decade of the rosary! Filthy feckers!

The End

Other books by S. Daly

Funny Feckin' Irish Jokes *Just .99cents*

30 Lessons I learned Before 30 *Just $1.99*

50 Epic gym hacks! *Just $1.99*

Keep turning for a sneak peek!

Funny Feckin' Irish Jokes!

By S. Daly

Table of Contents

Did ya hear the one about...

Did ya hear about the Irish boomerang?

It doesn't come back; it just sings songs about how much it wants to

Did you hear about the Irishmen who were asked to be a Jehovah witness?

They refused because they had not seen the accident

Did you hear about the Irish abortion clinic?

It has a 9 month waiting list

Did you hear about the Irishman that tried to blow up a car?

He burnt his mouth on the exhaust pipe

Did you hear Ireland's solved their unemployment problem?

You don't leave school till you are 65

Did you hear about the Irishman born with two left feet?

He went out one day to buy some Flip Flips...

Did you hear about the Irish attempt on Mt. Everest?

They ran out of scaffolding

Did you hear about the Irish newlyweds?

They sat up all night waiting for their sexual relations to arrive

Did you hear about the winner of the Irish beauty contest?

Me neither

Did you hear about the Irish pilot who crashed his helicopter?

He got cold so he turned off the fan

Did you hear about the Irish girl who asked her mammy for an encyclopaedia for Christmas?

Her mammy said 'No' and that she could walk to school like the rest of the kids

Did you hear the one about the two Irish boys who got a sledge for Christmas?

One of them used it for going down the hill and the other used it for going up!

Did you hear about the Irishman that had a penis transplant?

His hand rejected it!

Did you heard about the Irishman who was rushed to hospital?

He tried to drink a ship in a bottle